How to be su
following your conversion to
the Lord Jesus-Christ?

Dr Hubert Kayonda Ngamaba, PhD

How to be successful following your conversion to the Lord Jesus-Christ?

A series of teachings adapted to the realities of daily life, introduced by a servant of God, full of the Holy Spirit, a man of science converted to the Lord Jesus

Dr Hubert Kayonda Ngamaba, BSc(Hons), M.A., PhD

Scripture quotations are taken from the Holy Bible, King James, New International Version.

Grave la vision

www.gravelavision.com

DEDICATION

To all those who are born again Christian and willing to have a successful Christian life.
To my wife for her love and continuous support
To my lovely children, so they can be inspired.

ACKNOWLEDGMENTS

This Book would not have been published without the support, help, advice and encouragement from so many people. I would say I have been extremely blessed.

First, I would like to thank my God for absolute first class support.

I would like to thank Anderson and his wife for translating this book from French to English. I really appreciate their time and support.

I would like to thank my big brother Bishop Dr Emmanuel Soni Mukwenze for supporting and training me. I would like to thank Rev Pastor David Mabalu for coaching me as new Christian and Minister.

I would like to thank all members of the Ephrata Church Bolton for their support and encouragement.

I am extremely grateful to my wife, my best friend Fideline Mulenge who been hugely supportive and I would like to thank her for lifting my spirits during the difficult time. I would like to thank my children Esperant, El Gracia, Esther, Elysee and Benedict Kayonda for their love & providing an excellent family environment.

Finally, I will say: "Everything is possible for one who believes in Jesus-Christ." Mark 9:23

Contents

1 Redemption:
   1.1 Definition.
   1.2 The origin of sin.
   1.3 Death is the consequence of sin.
   1.4 The sacrifice of an animal instead of guilty man
   1.5 Redemption in the Old Testament
   1.6 Jesus Christ our Redeemer
   1.7   God accepts only the sacrifice of His only son Jesus Christ

2 New Birth
   2.1 Definition
   2.2 It is essential to be born again
   2.3 Why must man be born again?
   2.4 What happens after being born again?
   2.5 What must man do to be born again?

3 Receiving Christ
   3.1 Why do we receive Christ, and how?
   3.2 When can we receive Jesus Christ?
   3.3 Praying to receive Jesus Christ

1 Definition of prayer
2 Importance of prayer
3 Kinds of prayer
4 When to pray

Chapter 3: Angels, Satan, demons and the spiritual battle
page 29

Chapter 4: The Church and the fellowship   page 43

Chapter 5: Bearing witness   page 49

Introduction

It is in trying to help our brothers and sisters grow normally that we wanted to put at the disposal of Christians a series of Biblical teachings for today.

We are often shocked to notice some short-lived conversions of Christians with stunted growth in the faith.

When someone accepts Jesus Christ, he is obliged to know properly this Jesus to whom he has just given his life. And the knowledge which the new convert needs must be presented in simple but precise terms.
The new convert needs general training, but in few words and in a short amount of time, even if detailed knowledge must follow.

Faith comes from what one hears; that is why, after conversion the Christian must try and listen to good spiritual things, balanced and presented by Christians who have not only spiritual knowledge but also a training and occupation other than the pastorate.

Many questions find their answers in our manual; for example: Why do certain Christians no longer live with the zeal of the primitive Church?

What must one do so that Christians might control and cure certain key sectors of national or world economy?

Why do certain Christians not face up to corruption when they are called to cure it in the public sphere?

Why do certain Christians not face up to demonic attacks? Why do they not know how to make a difference in kindness and good conduct in the midst of their jobs or their home area? After conversion the new Christian needs a series of teachings on almost all aspects of daily life which will allow him or her to grow in faith and develop normally in his or her business.

We understood, as a man of science, Doctor in health psychology and theologian, that man lives according to what he believes, and that the environment in which we live has a serious impact on our growth as Christians. Furthermore the first teachings received after conversion must be balanced, well chosen and bestowed by people who give a good account of themselves, for the future of the new convert depends on it.

Many themes have been elaborated in our manual, beginning with redemption, new birth, conversion to the Lord Jesus, spiritual beings and spiritual warfare, the Church and the fellowship, bearing witness, baptism by water, the Holy Spirit, reading the word of God, achieving physical and moral health, work, as well as material and financial prosperity, knowing how to give, love of one's country, sanctification, and finally the return of Jesus Christ. These subjects are not the subjects of classic courses at a Bible college, but are useful matters for a new convert in a formative stage; why not for a former convert who wants a victorious life in Christ Jesus.

Chapter1   Redemption- forgiveness of sin – new birth – conversion to the Lord Jesus

1 Redemption:
   1.1 Definition.
   1.2 The origin of sin.
   1.3 Death is the consequence of sin.
   1.4 The sacrifice of an animal instead of guilty man
   1.5 Redemption in the Old Testament
   1.6 Jesus Christ our Redeemer
   1.7   God accepts only the sacrifice of His only son Jesus Christ

2 New Birth
   2.1 Definition
   2.2 It is essential to be born again
   2.3 Why must man be born again?
   2.4 What happens after being born again?
   2.5 What must man do to be born again?

3 Receiving Christ
   3.1 Why do we receive Christ, and how?
   3.2 When can we receive Jesus Christ?
   3.3 Praying to receive Jesus Christ

Chapter1   Redemption- forgiveness of sin – new birth – conversion to the Lord Jesus

1. REDEMPTION

Definition: Redemption is the payment of a ransom or price for the liberation of an individual. It is the payment of a price for the liberation of a slave.

Man makes himself a slave in the garden of Eden because of sin. In disobeying God, man was enslaved by giving in to the temptation of the devil (Genesis 3 v1, 6 and 19); hence the sin of man.

1.1 Definition of sin:

Sin is disobedience toward God; an act contrary to divine law; it is also an evil power reigning in the heart of man; original sin is the transgression of Adam, the first man, and by him all his human descendants have become sinful.

1.2 The origin of sin

The origin of mankind's sin starts with the disobedience of Adam and Eve according to Genesis 2: 16-17: "The Eternal God gave this command to the man: You will be able to eat all the trees of the garden; but you will not eat of the tree of the knowledge of good and evil, for the day when you eat of it, you will certainly die." The Bible tells us, "Satan taking the form of a serpent tempted the woman to disobey God's command; and the woman saw that the tree was good to eat and pleasing to one's sight, and that it was invaluable for opening up intelligence; she took of its fruit, and ate of it; she gave some also to her husband, who was close to her, and he ate of it." St. Paul:

"That is why, since by only one man sin entered the world, and by sin came death, and that death also spread to all mankind, because all have sinned, and are without the glory of God; it is through Jesus Christ that life entered the world." (Romans 5: 12, 21).

1.3. Death is the consequence of sin

"For you are dust, and you will return into dust" (Gen 3: !9); mankind died until this day because of his sinful state.

Romans 6:23 says that the wages of sin is death. But what kind of death? It is first of all about physical death, inflicted on all mankind; and spiritual death, destined for all those who have never received Jesus Christ.

1.4. The sacrifice of an animal instead of guilty man

God in His love instituted the sacrifice of an animal as a substitute for the man who was considered to be guilty. The Bible says in Leviticus 4.1-4 that a person who has sinned must offer to the Eternal God for the sin which he has committed, a young bull without fault, as an expiatory sacrifice. And he must put his hand on the head of the bull, whose throat he will cut in front of the Eternal God.

1.5. Redemption in the Old Testament

The Redeemer is he who pays back a ransom. Since the Old Testament, repayment was made either by a brother or by a close relative, for the freedom of the person who was a slave or who has given up his property or his own welfare. Leviticus 25.25 says "If your brother becomes poor and sells a portion of his property, he who has the right to pay back, his nearest relative, will sell some of his own goods and recoup what his brother had sold." Leviticus 25.48"There will be for him the right of repurchase after he has been sold; one of his brothers will be able to buy him back."

1.6. Jesus Christ our redeemer

The Bible says in Romans 3.23-24"For all have sinned and all are deprived of the glory of God; and they are freely justified by His grace, by the means of the redemption which is in Jesus Christ." And it adds, "Christ has repurchased us from the curse of the law, and He gives Himself for us, so as to redeem us from all iniquity. (Galatians 3.13, Titus 2.14). Jesus Christ is from now on our redeemer for having repurchased mankind from slavery to the devil by His death on the cross at Golgotha.

1.7. God accepts only the sacrifice of his only Son Jesus Christ

The New Testament underlines in the Letter to the Hebrews 10.5-7 "That is why Christ, coming into the world, says (to God the Father): You wanted neither sacrifice nor offering, but you have prepared a body for me; you have agreed on neither burnt offerings nor sacrifices for sin." Then he said, "See, I come, O God, to do your will." As God accepted neither sacrifice nor offering, it was necessary that a holy man, without sin, should die in the place of sinful man. That is why the Son of God was made man in taking a body to take away the sins of mankind; He who has no sin at all, so that by his freely-given grace we may obtain pardon for our sins (Heb.9.28, Romans 3.23-24).

2. NEW BIRTH

2.1 Definition

New birth is a spiritual birth which is made in a person aware after having understood and recognised that in Adam he or she was dead spiritually; that is to say the relationship between that person and God was severed. By new birth man repents by being aware of his sinful state; man is converted by changing direction or attitude; man changes thanks to a sincere repentance and a true conversion.

2.2 It is essential to be born again:

In John 3.3 Jesus Christ says: "If a man is not born again, he cannot see the kingdom of God." And he adds, "Do not be astonished that I have said to you, you must be born again (John 3.7)." There is no Christian life without new birth. As a child comes into the world by a physical birth, we become children of God by one and the same means, which is new birth (spiritual birth). Religion, baptism, morality or good works can not replace new birth; that is to say that one can become a child only after a new birth (Ephesians 2.8-9, John 3.7).

2.3 Why must man be born again?

a) Because he was born in sin and separated from God (Romans 7.18, Isaiah 39.2)

b) Because new birth is a divine requirement (John3.7).

c) Because it is through new birth that one begins the Christian life, one becomes a

child of God and one receives eternal life (John 1.12, 3.16).

2.4 What happens after being born again?

After having believed and received Jesus Christ as Lord and Saviour of his life, the Bible says that the Christian is saved (Luke 19.10), pardoned from all his sins ((Ephesians 1.7), becomes a child of God (John 1.12, Galatians 3.26), becomes a new creature and is reconciled with God (2 Corinthians 4.17, 5.18), capable of resurrection from among the dead (Ephesians 2.5-6).

2.5 What must one do to be born again?

It is necessary to answer God's invitation. That is what we call the part of man. In reality salvation is free, but God demands a willing acceptance from man knowledge of Jesus Christ as Lord and Saviour.

3. RECEIVING CHRIST

3.1. Why do we receive Christ and how?

We must receive Christ to be saved, because He has taken our place, and He died on the cross for our salvation (Romans 3, 23-24,; Galatians 3.13; Titus 2.14). The Bible says in 1 John 5.12 "He who has the Son has life; he who has not the Son of God does not have life." How can we receive Christ? It is by our faith inviting him into our life (Ephesians 2.8), for Jesus says in the Book of Revelation 3.20, "See, I stand at the door and knock. If someone hears my voice and opens the door, I will come into his house, and I will sup with him, and he with me." Also in Romans 10.9 "If you confess with your mouth the Lord Jesus, and if you believe in your heart that God has raised him from the dead, you will be saved." John 1.12 says "But to those who have received him, to those who believe in His name, Jesus Christ has given the power to become children of God. "

3.2. When can we receive Christ?

The appropriate moment for receiving Christ is "now, today, if you hear his voice, do not harden your hearts" Hebrews 3.7. Many people have seized this occasion in their lives, and have been pardoned, either by a sermon, on radio or television, by a chat with a friend at the office, at school...or even by a tract, sticker or hoarding, by being convinced through the Holy Spirit or by the Internet...

3.3. Praying to receive Jesus Christ.

It is better to express your commitment to the Lord by some words that are simple but profound and that show you are aware of what you are doing. In this prayer addressed to God it is important to thank God for His immeasurable love; to thank Jesus Christ for his death on the cross at Golgotha, taking your place, and to thank Him for His resurrection from the dead. Ask the Lord Jesus for forgiveness for having led your life without Him. Invite Jesus Christ to be the Lord or Master and Saviour of your life. Ask the Holy Spirit to fill you and accompany you each day. Tell the Lord you are concerned to want to grow in the faith and to inform others about the love of God.

Chapter2: Prayer

1　Definition of prayer
2　Importance of prayer
3　Kinds of prayer
4　When to pray
5　How to pray?
6　Where can we pray?
7　When and how often must one pray?
8　To whom can we pray, and for whom can we pray?
9　 Prayer and fasting.
10　Spiritual dryness

Chapter 2: Prayer

1. *Definition of prayer.* Prayer is a direct and spontaneous expression from man to God. It is a dialogue, and intimate conversation between God and His dearly-beloved children; it is a mutual discussion between man and God (Exodus 33.12-17). Prayer is offering to God through Jesus Christ a spiritual worship in a humble attitude. But beware: prayer is not a science, a talent or a mystical initiation, but rather a personal and lively relationship between the Christian and his heavenly Father. Some people or pagans make an appeal to a divinity, to an invisible being who they consider supreme, to spirits, saints, ancestors, by incantations and prayers; these are inadmissible practices and are forbidden.

2. *The importance of prayer:* During his earthly life Jesus Christ not only ordered us to pray, but also demonstrated the importance of prayer by his life of prayer (Luke 18.1-8). To pray allows us practically to express our love and trust in God, and to externalise our feelings for Him as well as to bear witness to God. Prayer allows us renew our commitment and to show our dependence on, and submission to, God. Prayer is a sure and solid shelter against attacks, traps and temptations, both demonic and human. Prayer prepares us to be able to confront difficult situations. Prayer immunises us against all the bad carnal desires, against pride, for our personality has a tendency to do evil or to be boastful. Prayer is a means by which we can unburden ourselves completely (Mat.11.28-30).

Prayer is a sacred duty, and from this fact, we have a privilege and responsibility to offer a sacrifice of prayer for the peace and salvation of the world.

3. *Kinds of prayer:*

> a) The prayer of praise and adoration
>
> b) The prayer of repentance
>
> c) The prayer of gratitude
>
> d) The prayer of supplication and intercession.

a) The prayer of praise and adoration: Praise is an expression of admiration for God because of his benefits towards us. It can be done in words as well as songs. Praise is an individual and voluntary activity which expresses the honour, glory and dignity of He whom one praises. We praise God for his benefits, and adore Him for what He is. Adoration is the fact of adoring. To adore God is to give Him worship in His honour, that is to say paying Him a service in magnifying him and showing Him our deep love and complete submission to Him by offering one's self and one's goods. Adoration is due only to a divinity; in our case it is destined for our God, the All-Powerful. All adoration to another divinity whether spiritual, material, human or ideological, other than Jehovah God, is idolatry. Adoration is the route par excellence for entering into the presence of God, and praise prepares our feelings for adoration. The aim of praise is to lead us to adoration. That is why it is very necessary to choose songs or hymns that will lead people to adore. The Hebrew word most often used for expressing adoration in the Old Testament means "bow down" (Genesis 18.2), but in the New Testament adoration means an act of respect with regard to God. God creates man for His own pleasure, and that is what He expects from His creature. Praise and adoration are an individual and voluntary act that expresses the honour, glory and dignity of the One whom one praises.

Why do we adore and praise God? It is because of His glory (His honour, His power, His majesty and His greatness) Psalm 148, Isaiah 24.14., His nobility (the wonder one feels at His excellence) Psalm 11.4, His holiness (which is perfect, putting him apart, different from all creatures from the point of view of his moral attributes), His wisdom (Daniel 2.20), His goodness (His love, His truth, His indulgence, His mercy and His faithfulness) Psalm 107.8, His immensity (Psalm 150.2), His marvellous works and His great deeds on high (Psalm 92.6, 150.1, 103.1,2), His judgements (Psalm 98.8).

b) *The prayer of repentance:*

Repentance is an internal suffering produced by a conviction that one has sinned, and this internal suffering must be accompanied by a deep desire to change (Acts2.37-38). A pagan can repent in order to come to Christ, and a Christian can repent throughout his life for having sinned. Repentance precedes the pardoning of sins. The prayer of repentance is the prayer in the course of which the soul of a Christian is humbled before the holy and just God, to obtain mercy and favour by a clean confession and a return to the Lord.

c) The prayer of thanksgiving: is a prayer of gratitude, and thanks for salvation and benefits that regenerate man has just enjoyed from God. 1 Thessalonians 5.18, Ephesians 5.20.

d) The prayer of supplication: There are three kinds of the prayer of supplication: requests, petitions and intercessions

Requests are demands made to a person in authority who has the power to decide; in our case it is addressing a request to the great King, the Sovereign Lord (Ephesians 6.18-20).

Petitions are requests addressed to God under the form of a plea asked while expounding a problem. The Christian is called on to submit a case to the Lord Jesus in prayer while formulating a request or by exhibiting an intention in his favour, which is to say claiming a right before the Lord (Acts 4.21-31).

Intercessions are prayers made in favour of someone. In Greek it is invoking God in favour of others, while in Hebrew it is imploring God in favour of someone. This aspect of prayer demands first of all compassion and affection, thoughtfulness in favour of those who are in need. God needs intercessors, people who stand up in the breach to pray for the nations (Ezekiel 22.30, Isaiah 59.16).

Example of an intercession programme of intercession:

Monday: pray for families: for love between spouses, divorced couples, children's studies, and their turning towards the Lord Jesus;

Tuesday: pray for missionaries, students on missionary training; their next expeditions;

Wednesday: intercede for politicians and administrative authorities; management of public affairs;

Thursday: pray for God's servants and local churches

Friday: pray for the expansion of the gospel, campaigns of evangelism, welcoming new converts; any place can be good for prayer.

Saturday: pray for teachers in primary and secondary schools and in universities; people concerned about finding jobs, the unemployed, local initiatives;

Sunday: Intercede for the sick, orphans, prisoners and institutions involved in social care.

5 *How to pray; what positions to adopt:* Prayer is an intimate conversation between God and the Christian. It is a state of mind; also the heart is in a good relationship with God; so the body will be ready and flexible to adapt itself or to submit itself to practical positions under the influence of the Holy Spirit. Every Christian must adopt a position which seems convenient to his or her physical state, but he must be also attentive to all positions so that the Holy Spirit may be able to breathe into him. From all that has been said, the teaching is that the practice must correspond to the internal reality. Many positions can be used during prayer:

- prostration, Joshua 7.6;
- kneeling, the hands raised to heaven, 1 Kings 8.54, Psalm 77.3

- hands held towards the temple, Psalm 28.2;
- the head between the knees, Luke 22.41;
- standing with eyes raised, 1 Kings 8.22-23;
- simply kneeling, Luke 22.40-41;
- lying down, 2 Kings 4.33-35.

6 *Where can we pray?* Any place can be good for prayer, provided that the human mind remains in communion with the Lord, away from all distraction and lack of concentration. That is why some people advise closing one's eyes, but in an office, for example, of many serving colleagues, it will be impossible for you sometimes to close your eyes. The more we let the Holy Spirit enter into us, and the more the mind and soul rise into the presence of God, the more we forget our environment or attach no more importance to it (1Timothy 2.8).

7 *When and how often must one pray?* The New Testament, like the Old Testament, gives the possibility of discovering that the notion of time is a subject for liberty of choice in regard to hours of prayer or of a calendar for personal, collective or national prayer, and finally of a timetable that considers our circumstances. Of course divine directives ought to be encouraged. It is necessary to know how to maintain and cultivate an attitude of prayer, and to give oneself a discipline in respect of hours for prayer. In the Bible we have cases of people who have had the habit of praying at certain moments in the day. During the morning (Psalm 5.1-4), at noon and at night (Psalm 55.17-18), during night and day (Psalm 88.2-3)and every time that one feels the

need (Philippians 4.6) are the different times that one can give to prayer.

8 Whom to pray to and whom to pray for. To whom can we address our prayers? The   Bible teaches us that prayer can only be connected with the person of the Eternal, our creator God and Father of Jesus Christ. It is therefore forbidden to address any prayer to another divinity, a saint, the dead or ancestors...for God can never give his glory to idols (Exodus 20.1-5).

Whom to pray for? We must pray for everyone (1Timothy 2.1-8), including our brothers and sisters in Christ (Ephesians 6.18). We must pray for people in authority and for political leaders, for our family, our church and nation, for people in general, our enemies, and for those who persecute us (Matt.5.38-48). It is forbidden to pray for the dead (Heb.9.27, Es.8.19). It is also forbidden to pray for deposed angels, for Lucifer and even for the angels of God (Revelation 22.8-9, Luke 4.5-8).

9   *Prayer with fasting:*
   a) What is fasting? The word "fasting" comes from the Hebrew; it is an exercise of   abstinence during which a person or group of Christians humble their souls and bodies before God in prayer. Fasting is an abstention from food or something else that you consider to be important; for example sexual relationships for married people. Fasting is mentioned for the first time in Judges 20.26, and then mentioned in many other verses in the Bible. We fast to humble ourselves before God because of our sin, to pray and invoke the Eternal so that He will intervene in a difficult situation (2 Chronicles 20.1-4, Acts

14.23). In Israel fasting was first of all circumstantial; then during their captivity the Jews are going to organise solemn and ritual fasts, and fasting became a form of piety without spiritual value; so Isaiah in reaction will introduce real fasting (Isaiah 58.3-9, Matthew 6.16-18, Luke 18.10-12).

b) *Kinds of fasts:* Normal fasting is abstention from food, but the Christian leads a normal life, avoiding putting on a sad expression; he perfumes himself and washes his face (Matthew 6.16-18). Partial fasting is also called dieting; the Christian does it with the support of a little food, or a light meal (Daniel 10.3). Absolute fasting is done without the support of any food (Exodus 34.28, Matthew 4.2). Absolute fasting is done away from all human contacts with the power to distract.

c) *Reasons for fasting in the Old and the New Testaments.* One might fast to express a profound grief or to prevent and turn away God's anger from His people. One can do it to express repentance for sin (Jonas 3.7). The Lord Jesus Christ respects fasting while reproaching the ritual and hypocrisy surrounding fasting (Matthew 6.16-18). Jesus begins his ministry with fasting (Luke 4.1-2).

10. *Spiritual dryness:*
   a. definition: It is a normal period in the life of a Christian, a period in which the Christian will feel himself unmotivated and discouraged. There is an absence of intense prayer and an absence of fellowship.

b. cause: Spiritual dryness is often due to sin that has not been confessed; to silence in front of pagan injunctions criticising Jesus Christ or criticising the Church; to the envy of pagans (Psalm 73.1-16); to bad company, to the fact of always being in the company of pagans; to the action of demons on the life of the Christian due to negligence; to the loss of a life filled with the Holy Spirit.

c. How can one come out of it? By going into the presence of God with a sincere repentance; seeing more the final fate of the wicked than contemplating their apparent prosperity; (Psalm 73.2-3,16-19); fasting and prayer; breaking with bad company; believing in and confessing the victory of Jesus Christ; asking God to fill you with the Holy Spirit (Ephesians 6.18).

Chapter 3: Angels, Satan, demons and the spiritual battle

1 Angels
2 Satan
3 Demons
4 The spiritual warfare

Chapter 3: Angels, Satan, demons, deliverance and the spiritual warfare

1   Angels:

An angel, in Greek, means someone who is sent, a messenger. The Bible teaches us about the existence of angels in the Old Testament and the New Testament. Jesus Christ himself taught on this subject.

a)   *Their origin:* They have been pulled from nothingness by the complete power of God; they are spiritual beings.

b)   *Their nature:* If man is dichotomous (material and spiritual) the angels are spiritual beings not possessing a physical body. They are different from men, and are not limited by physical or natural conditions. That is why they can appear at will in any place and in the winking of an eye. They also have the possibility of taking human form in certain divine missions (to Abraham, for instance Genesis 18.1-4, 19.1-2). They are immortal and have no sex (Matthew 22.30, Luke 20.30-35, Mark 12.25). There are great numbers of them (Psalm 68. 18, Matthew 26.53). Their power is unimaginable (2 Kings 19.35); they have their place around the throne of God (Revelation 5.11, 7.11). Each Christian has at least one angel of God who camps around him to snatch him from all danger (Psalm 34.8). Angels have a relationship with men as "spirits in the service of God, sent to exercise a ministry in favour of those who must inherit salvation" (Hebrews 1.14). Their ministry relates in large measure to physical protection and to the wellbeing of the children of God (1 Kings 19.5, Daniel 6.22). Angels observe us (1 Corinthians

4.9), and this surveillance must influence our conduct. Man was made to be only "a little lower than the angels", and by His incarnation Christ has taken this inferior place "for a little time" (Hebrews 2.7, Psalm 8.5-6) to raise the Christian above the angels in the heavenly places in Jesus Christ (Hebrews 2.9-10, Ephesians 2.6). The angels will accompany Christ during His second coming (Matthew 25.31), and to them will be entrusted the preparation for the judgement of individuals from every nation (Matthew 13.30, 39, 41-42). The kingdom of God will not be subject to the angels, but to Christ and his followers (Hebrews 2.7).

c) *Classification:* As order is the first point of law in heaven, angels are classified according to their ranks and activities. Also we have this order:

d) *The angel of the Lord:* is a term used in the Bible when one wants to make mention of God Himself. Unlike the other angels the Angel of the Eternal is presented as He to whom we owe adoration, He who has the power to pardon, and sometimes called Jehovah (Genesis 31.11-13, Exodus 3.2-6).

e) *The archangels:* the most elevated class of all angels. There are three: MICHAEL, GABRIEL and LUCIFER. Their roles are also defined:
Lucifer was busy with adoration and praise;
Gabriel was busy with exterior relationships and information; he transmitted divine messages to men (Luke 1.36).
Michael: is a reckless warrior who always intervenes in combat to deliver the people of God. After Lucifer's

rebellion, God never raised another angel, but created man, and entrusted to him his ministry of praise and adoration. Also, when man praises and adores, the angels make their adoration just the same.

f) *Angels of the nations:* They are heavenly principalities with a mission to guard the nations to which they are assigned, as Michael is the angel of Israel according to Daniel 12.

g) *Cherubim: (Genesis 3.24, Exodus 25.22)* seem to be raised into the rank of angels. They intervene in what concerns judgement, the chastisement that God inflicts. They are a class of warrior angels who specialise in military expeditions and who have fought many times in favour of Israel. They occupy an elevated rank of angels, and it is among them that the archangels come. They also have business in God's plan or design, in his chastisement and in His plan of redemption.

h) *The seraphim:* (Isaiah 6.2-3) have as their mission lying prostrate before the throne of God in praise and adoration

i) *Characters and tasks:* Angels are obedient to the will of God, and they accomplish what is asked of them in their mission (Luke 1.28, 35). They have reverence (Nehemiah 9.6), and adore Christ (Hebrews 1.6). They have wisdom (2 Samuel 14, 17), and humility (Ps.103.20); they tell us that there is no humility without obedience, and no obedience without humility. They make announcements (Luke 1.10-11). Angels give warnings (Matthew 2.14), and instructions (Matthew 28.2-6, Acts 10.3, Daniel 4.13-

14), and revelations (Acts 7.53, Galatians 2.2, Daniel 9.21-27).

j) *The ministry of angels to Christ:* Angels predicted the birth of Jesus Christ (Luke 1.26-33); they protected the infant Jesus Christ (Matthew 2.13). An angel was sent to the garden of Gethsemane while He prayed there (Luke 22.43). Angels rolled away the stone at His tomb (Matthew 28.2), and announced His resurrection (Matthew 28.2); they also predicted His return (Acts 1.9-11). Angels will sound a trumpet (1 Thessalonians 4.16), and will connect together the elect from the four corners of the earth (Matthew 24.31). They always adore Jesus and God the Father (Matthew 4.11).

k) *The ministry of angels to the faithful and the nations: (Hebrews 1.7, 14):* They come to assist us, and work at our side, or are collaborators in distancing obstacles and in bringing us God's blessings. This collaboration is influenced by our sanctification (Psalm 34.8, Daniel 6.22, 2 Kings 6.17). They are interested in the ministry of adoration which Christians make, and come to take part (1 Corinthians 11.10). They are interested in the effort of evangelisation by Christians (Luke 13.14, Acts 10.6-7). They watch over the bodies of the just after their death (Jude 9). Michael specially watches over Israel. Angels execute judgements with regard to faithless nations (Genesis 19), and fight the enemies of the children of God (Exodus 23.20-23). They will be involved in the final judgement and the great retribution (Revelation 8.9).

2. Satan:

2.1. The origin of Satan: The devil is one of God's creatures; he comes from the angelic world, and was created good and holy. At creation he wore the name of Lucifer, which means bright star, son of the dawn (Isaiah 14.12-16). The Bible declares that at creation he was raised in glory and was perfect in wisdom and beauty, and was busy leading praise and adoration in heaven. That is why since his fall he has done everything to make men adore him instead of God, for he knew the value of adoration.

2.2. His rebellion (Isaiah 14.12-140 and his fall: The devil rebelled against God's authority by creating sin in himself, making himself also equal to God. Christians must avoid making themselves equal to God, or to the Good Shepherd, for fear of falling into Satan's trap. By rebelling, Lucifer in his rebellion swept along an important number of angels. Hunted along with his acolytes from the presence of God, he kept guard over the gifts that he had, and from then on would be called Satan.

2.3. The personality of Satan: Satan is not a simple force of influence as some people believe. The devil pulls his origin from the angelic world. Satan was an angel of God, and since his fall he lives a spiritual life which has a personality; that is to say he has a will, intelligence, knowledge, but unfortunately aimed at doing evil (1 CorInthians 11.14).

2.4. The different names of Satan:
Satan: one who opposes God, His adversary;
the devil: the slanderer;

Beelzebul from the Greek Beel-Zebub (2 Kings 1.2) chief Lord of the Flies; that is to say prince of the demons;
Bélial: the wicked one;
Apollyon: the destroyer (Revelation 9.11);
Leviathan: the sea monster (Psalm 104.26).

2.5. His titles and representations:

The crafty one (Matthew 6.13), the usurper, the evil one, the tempter, the prince of this world (John 12.31), the prince of the power of the air ((Ephesians 2.2), the prince of darkness, the god of this age (2 Corinthians 4.4), the accuser of our brethren (Revelation 12.10), the ancient serpent (Revelation 12.9), the dragon (Revelation 12.17), the angel of light, the shining star.

2.6. The nature of the devil:

6.1 Characteristics: He is a creature of God; he was created and has limits (Exodus 28.14); He is a spiritual being with neither flesh nor blood (Ephesians 6.12); he belongs to the order of cherubim, and was the most elevated of all angelic creatures (Exodus 28.12).

6.2 Traits of personality: he is a murderer (John 10.10), the father of lies (John 8.44), the one who accuses our brotherhood of sin, (Revelation 12.10), a confirmed sinner (1 John 3.8), the opponent of all that is good and true.

6.3: His limitations: being a creature of God, he has limits, for he is not omnipresent (he is not everywhere); he is not omniscient (he does not know everything); he is not omnipotent (he is not able to do everything) and he is not infinite (Job 1.12). Finally he can be resisted by Christians (James 4.7).

2.7. God's judgement of Satan:

He was chased from heaven and hastily put on earth (Exodus 28.16-17). God's judgement was pronounced in the garden of Eden (Genesis 3.11-15) and at the cross of Golgotha (John 12.30-31, Colossians 2.14-15); with the final judgement his acolytes and he will be thrown into the eternal lake of fire (Revelation 20.10).

2.8. What the devil has done to Christ, and what he does to Christians and to the nations;

As predicted since Genesis 3.15, the devil has tempted certain people to kill the infant Jesus (Matthew 2.13); he tempted Jesus – Christ in the desert (Matthew 4); he will use several people to prevent Jesus from achieving the work of the cross; he will possess Judas so that he will commit high treason; he is the tempter of Christians (Acts 5.3); he accuses Christians, and holds up their work and ministry (1 Thessalonians 2.18); the devil pushes Christians towards carnal and immoral passions (1 Corinthians 5.1, 7.5); he works up persecutions and afflictions against Christians (Revelation 2.10); he causes natural disasters; he controls political power and the business world; he blinds the intelligence of unbelievers by making them sceptical about the faith (Luke 8.12); he collects together all the nations of the world ready for the war of Armageddon (Revelation 16.13-14)

3. Demons and the organisation of the world of darkness:

3.1 Demons, their existence and origin:

Demons are spiritual beings with their origin in the angelic world. They are angels that the devil has dragged into his rebellion and who were deposited with him (Revelation 12.7).

3.2 The activities of these demons:

It is in trying to be everywhere that the devil organises his demons into sharing various activities. They are prepared to destroy humanity with the main object of fighting man to destroy him, for they have no will to seek the happiness of man. They are grouped into classes each with a special object, such as warrior demons, or demons promoting greed or gluttony, immodesty, indecency or quarrelling.

3.3 Organisation into class or speciality:

In trying fully to control the world and impose his rule over it, the devil classifies demons into:

a) *Dominations or principalities*, which is to say: leaders (Colossians 2.10, 3.15);

b) *Authorities* with the power to govern (Colossians 2.10-15);

c) *Princes of darkness* who overpower human beings, and who exercise authority over them.

d) *Evil spirits:* spiritual forces who live above our heads (Ephesians 6.12).

3.4 Their ministries: thwarting God's plan; popularising and spreading Satan's authority by achieving his will; Christians must fight them (Ephesians 6.11-12); God can use demons to achieve His aims (2 Chronicles 18.19-21);

they inflict illnesses, but beware – some illnesses exist in the absence of good hygiene! They take possession of human beings and animals; they create and spread false doctrines (2Timothy 4.10); that is why those who hold to true doctrine must spread it around as well as possible. They sow disorder and blind people so that those people cannot believe the gospel (2 Corinthians 4.4).

3.5 How may we discover demons? We have two methods:

a) The supernatural method: by the gift of discerning spirits. This gift allows us to know what acts in the mind of such a man or such a thing or that works in such a group or family or district (1 Corinthians 12.10);

b) The natural method: one can discover demons thanks to Christian experience; they may be due to mental troubles in the victim (forgetfulness, madness, epilepsy, headaches); demons love to use harmful language (lying, blasphemy, cursing, easy abuse, gossip, mockery); they can create disordered sexual life (masturbation, incest, fornication, homosexuality, lesbianism, adultery, paedophilia, concubinage, prostitution); addiction to alcohol or drugs and religiosity (exaggerated devotion to a given false religion at any price).

3.6 How demons operate:

So that they operate and express themselves, demons have needs and a body (human or animal). Demons can either possess or oppress someone or even haunt someone.

a) Possession is the fact of being entirely dominated by an impure mind. The life of the victim is under the domination of Satan and his agents. A Christian cannot be possessed.

b) Oppression is an exterior influence of demons who possess someone or something so that they lose control. In this case the demon does not inhabit the person, but influences him by means of exterior thoughts that bring to heel the conscience of the person.

c) Obsession is an effort of demons to act on someone in order to push them into activities that thought and conscience condemn but that they do not know how to avoid.

4. The spiritual battle:

4.1 How demons enter into man:

It is by gates of entry that demons enter into man. Among these are: sin: the demon pushes man to commit sin. This consummate sin, when not confessed, allows sin to enter into man;

By the circumstances of life: such as infants without parental protection;

By heredity: when the chief of a family signs a pact with the devil, he makes him enter the whole genital line of his family, even several generations afterwards (1 Peter 1.18);

By sexual perversion: knowing the importance of the sexual organ the devil falsifies and trivialises the use of this organ (Romans 1.24-32); for example masturbation, immodesty, adultery, homosexuality, incest, rape, sexual attraction towards dead bodies, bestiality, paedophilia and voyeurism.

4.2 Deliverance and its value:

This is the method by which demons are chased from a body, a house or a tree. It is not, however, a remedy in itself, but it is however an important part of man's restoration. True deliverance comes from the word of God (Hebrews 4.12). It is difficult to grow spiritually if you are not delivered. That is why deliverance is indispensable. The delivered Christian sees himself blessed in life, he is sensitive to the Holy Spirit, and such a Christian manifests the fruits of the Holy Spirit.

4.3 The different stages of deliverance:

After having noted some suspicious signs, and sometimes after a treatment of the soul, it is necessary to be ready to be delivered, as that takes some time; one must know that one is in Christ, who is more than a conqueror, and try to bring someone else to Christ in repentance and renunciation; the prayer of invoking the name of Jesus Christ is necessary, for the adoration and praise of Him breaks the chains of sin; one must give orders to the demons, and not to negotiate with them even if they resist.

Remarks: Refer always to the victory of Jesus Christ; stay attached to the word of God, for demons easily lie. Cut all links and pacts signed even by ancestors of the victim; cut all suspect threads at the belt and at the chest of the victim, but use a sister in Christ to untie certain threads at the homes of women; avoid distraction during the deliverance; quote certain verses or declarations in the victory of Jesus Christ to the victim; be more attentive to the presence of Jesus than to the presence of the demons.

4.4 Why and until when the spiritual battle must be fought

After the man or woman accepts Christ as Saviour and Lord of his or her life, he or she has enrolled himself into the celestial army of God. By this membership, the devil becomes from now on the sworn enemy of the Christian. His aim is to turn the Christian back, and to prevent him from inheriting eternal life. That is why the Bible recommends us to resist the devil (James 4.7). Even to plant a church you must know the spiritual state of the place, the demons who dominate the milieu, so as to deprive them of their control (Colossians 2.15).

Testimony: on the deliverance of one young person. One day on a walk I saw a distracted mental patient, whom certain people would abusively call a madman, beside a notice board, and he fixed his gaze on me, but knowing that he was abnormal, I might have quite simply avoided him. To my great surprise, after having crossed the road, the man said to me, "Pray for me"; so, led by the Holy Spirit, I put this question to the man, "Where do you live?" He will give me an address that I will write down, with the promise of meeting him at 3 o'clock in the afternoon next day. The following day, after a preparation of prayer and fasting, we met with a young brother in Christ. Although it was difficult for his parents to receive us, we convinced them to enter into contact with their child. Coming to a standstill we will learn that the young man used to be a student. After we had led him to Christ, thanks to a very short sermon, thank God, he accepts Jesus Christ as Lord and Saviour of his life. We ended the meeting with a prayer for deliverance for him. We had to wait a day so that his parents might note a clean transformation in their child, who some days afterwards returned to his studies. His parents, who had never seen such things, wanted to give us some precious gifts, and they would consider us to be supermen. We of course refused these presents, and by the grace of God explained to them what Jesus Christ is capable of doing.

Chapter 4: The Church and the fellowship

1 The Church

    1.1 Definition of the Church

    1.2 Kinds of church

    1.3 Characteristics of the Church

    1.4 The symbolisms of the Church and their connections with Christ

    1.5 Why go to church?

    1.6 Can you change church?

2 Fellowship in a local church

    2.1 Definition

    2.2 Where can one live out this fellowship?

    2.3 The subjects we can talk about during meetings

Chapter 4   The church and the fellowship

1. The church

1.1 Definition of the church: from the Greek "ekklesia" meaning "called out of" or "those who are called out of", an assembly of people called into a place to adore God.

1.2 Kinds of church: There are two kinds of church in existence: the worldwide church which is the body of Christ, and the local church.

a)   The worldwide body of Christ's church (Matthew 16.18): It is the mystical union of Christians of all the ages, whose head is Jesus Christ. This body is not visible at the moment. This church is commonly called the universal church, constituted of Christians regenerated since Pentecost until the Ascension. As for the number of members, only Christ knows that, but Revelation 7.9 tells us that there are myriads of every language, every tribe, every nation and people who make up this church.

b) The local church: (Matthew 18.15-17, 1 Corinthians 16.19). This is a specific group of people in a local environment, earthly and definable, who are united in the name of the Lord Jesus Christ. The local church is the visible and temporal expression of the body of Christ in a given geographical aspect. The local assembly is a group of believers professing Christ who unites them and organises them with the aim of achieving God's will, celebrating the Lord Jesus Christ and living in communion with each other and with Him. Local churches differ one from the other, perhaps at the level of administration or practices as to the interpretation of certain biblical passages (for example as to the practice of praying, the sacraments, or dress). In these churches, one can find the children of God born again, false Christians living still in sin, ravishing wolves sent by the devil (Acts 20.26-30).

1.3 Characteristics of the church:

1. The church must be a victorious army against Satan and the world;

2. The church must live as a loving fellowship;

3. The church of Jesus Christ must be a place where the word of God is really   preached, where the Spirit works, and where Jesus Christ is adored.

1.4 The symbols of the church and their connections with Christ:

The church is a body of several members of whom Jesus Christ is the head

(Colossians 1.18, 1 Corinthians 12.12).

The church is the temple or edifice built with many stones, of which Jesus Christ is the cornerstone (Ephesians 2.20).

The church is a flock of many sheep, of which Jesus Christ is the shepherd (John10.10).

The church is a nation of many citizens, of whom Jesus Christ is the Lord (1 Peter 2.9).

The church is a family of many brothers, of whom Jesus Christ is the eldest (Colossians 1.15, 18).

The church is a vine of many branches, of which Jesus Christ is the trunk (John 15.2,5).

The church is an army of many soldiers, of whom Jesus Christ is the garrison commander (Revelation 17.14, 19.16, Joshua 5.14-15, 2 Timothy 2, 3).

The church is a kingdom with many princes, of whom Jesus Christ is the king (Luke19.12-19).

The church is a royal priesthood, for whom Jesus Christ is the Supreme Sacrifice (1 Peter 2.9, Revelation 1.5-6).

The church is a bride, of whom Jesus Christ is the husband (Ephesians 5.31-32, Revelation 21.1-10).

1.5   Why go to church?

It is to listen to the word of God, through pastors and other people who are servants of God; to live the life of loving fellowship, for a new Christian has a need to discover other converted brothers and sisters, and to appreciate and imitate good habits; and there is a need to find another structure where men and women adore God, a place without injuries, frauds, drugs or disputes. It is a misfortune to find certain worldly practices within a church; but that can be explained by the fact that the local church contains not only committed Christians, but also people who are mere babes spiritually, and some unconverted people (non-Christians).   This loving fellowship answers the preoccupation of the Lord who says in 1 Corinthians 15.33, "Do not forget that bad company corrupts good manners". The church exists also as a rock in the advancement of the work of God with its talents, gifts and offerings, and to share a meal with the Lord, the Holy Communion.

1.6 Can you change the church?

Replying to this question, I would love to come again to one of the characteristics of the church. The church of Jesus Christ must be a place where the word of God is really preached, and where the Holy Spirit works and where Jesus Christ is adored. Therefore if your church does not answer to this characteristic, and if you are convinced that your contribution cannot change anything, and that this state of things means that you cannot grow in your faith, I advise you to leave that church, and to find another church where the Gospel is really preached. I am sure that many belong to such and such church because their parents or grandparents are members there.

2. The fellowship in a local church:

Acts 2.41-43: The Bible tells us that those who accepted His message were baptised; and in that day the number of the disciples increased to about three thousand souls. They persevered in the teaching of the apostles, in the fellowship, in the breaking of bread and in prayers. Fear seized each one of them, and many wonders and miracles were done by the apostles."

2.1 Definition: the word "communion" comes from the Latin word "communio", which is a union in the same faith; otherwise called "communion of the faithful" or "loving fellowship". But the communion of saints is a spiritual communion of all Christians living and dead.

2.2 Where can one live out this fellowship? It can be lived out at church, during our various meetings for instruction; apart from churchgoing, by visits, encouragement, for example during the celebration of the birthday anniversary of a child, during break at school, or during a coffee break at a church service.

2.3 What subjects can we talk about during our meetings?
Sharing the word of God; thinking about our plans and our business affairs; planning evangelisation strategies in a service or at school, or even in a different culture to yours (for example a mission to foreigners living in our town); discussing subjects around the choice of Christian engagements between boys and girls; organising meetings: debates on vital subjects like sexuality, sexually transmissible illnesses, homework and the rights of children, limitation on pregnancies, elections, success in business, initiating small plans of development...; planning guided visits and excursions for members of the church according to age or profession.

Chapter 5: Bearing witness

1 Some examples of Christian witness
2 Why witness to Christ?
3 What message to witness to?
4 When to bear witness?
5 What means are used?

Chapter 5:   Bearing witness

1. *Some examples of Christian testimony:*
   a. Jesus' meeting with the Samaritan woman (John 4.4-42): verses 28, 29 and 30 tell us that the Samaritan left her pitcher and went into the town to invite the inhabitants to come and see the man who has sounded her mind.   And through her, many Samaritans began to believe in Jesus.
   b. The cure of two blind men (Matthew 9.27-31): despite Jesus' forbidding them to spread the word about His healing them, and they refused to stop talking about it.
   c. The curing of a man who had limped and been shaky since birth before the temple in Jerusalem (Acts 3.3-12):

      v.6: in the name of Jesus of Nazareth, get up and walk;

      v.8: with a leap he was standing and began to walk. He entered with them into   the temple, walking and praising God.   And thanks to this miracle Peter announced the news of Jesus to the madman who ran after them.

2. *Why testify to Christ?*

   The Bible says in Romans 10.14 "How therefore will they believe in Him of whom they have not heard anyone speak?"   That is why other people listen and believe in the Lord. It is for future rewards (Daniel 12.3): those who announce the word of God to the multitudes will shine like stars. It is to obey the order of the Lord,

Who tells us to go and make disciples of all nations ((Matthew 28.19).

3. *To what message do we bear witness?*
We must say to His followers what Christ has done in their lives; your conversion, or your transformation, your physical healing or your peace of mind, and the pardon from which you benefit. You can refer to a Biblical passage, according to circumstances, preach or exhort someone. As a basis of discussion you can advise your friends to imitate you or imitate a certain brother or sister in Christ.

4. *When do we bear witness?* The Bible recommends us in 2 Timothy 4.2 to preach the Word on every occasion, whether the time is favourable or not. But I advise you to seize the opportunity.

5. *What means are used?*

Word of mouth: direct contact is often effective (evangelisation person to person);
Spoken word during great public meetings or a great assembly (with or without a microphone);
Radio, television, internet: an effective way to reach a large number;
Treatises, posters, evangelistic books etc

Chapter 6: Baptism by water

1 Definition
2 The practice of baptism by water is at the heart of history
3 Different forms of administration of baptism in water
4 When to be baptised?
5 In whose name must we be baptised?
6 The meaning of baptism
7 What water is used, and who has the right to be baptised

Chapter 6   Baptism by water

1. Definition: literally baptism means immersion or bathing or even washing one's self.

2. The practice of baptism by water throughout history:
    John the Baptiser: in the New Testament, the practice of baptism by water was introduced under the ministry of John the Baptiser who practised "the baptism of repentance for the forgiveness of sins" (Mark 1.4, Luke 3.3).

    Jesus Christ: Christ, although he did not need to repent, was nevertheless himself baptised by John (Matthew 3.13-17). He wanted to prove by this act His identification with humanity. Before his ascension, the Lord Jesus gave to His disciples the order to preach the Gospel in the whole world, and to baptise in the name of the Father, the Son and the Holy Spirit all those who believed in this message of salvation (Matthew 28.19, Mark 16.15-16).

    Pentecost and the primitive church: After the day of Pentecost, the commandment of Jesus Christ on baptism was observed by the primitive church (Acts 2.38, 41; 8.12-13; 22.13-16). Therefore since apostolic times baptism has been practised by the Christian church.

3. Different forms of administration of baptism in water:
    In the course of the history of the church, baptism has been administered in three ways, but only one of these ways is valid and Biblical. The different forms are:

Baptism by aspersion: that is to say pouring some drops of water on the head, practised by the Roman Catholic Church;

Baptism by infusion: that is to say spreading water on the head; "infusion" comes from the Latin "infundare", which means pouring or sprinkling on something. This form of baptism had to appear quite soon (second century), as there was little depth of water in the Middle East, and following the secret nature of Christian life due to persecution. According to the history of the church, this practice was authorised accidentally and it was recommended to pour water three times on a person's head.

Baptism by immersion, which is to say plunging into water (Matthew 3.13-17), was practised by John the Baptiser and Jesus Christ in the River Jordan; it is the only one, according to my opinion, that one can recommend in church.

4. When should one be baptised?

The Bible is clear: baptism comes just after conversion to Christianity, after having   received Jesus Christ as personal Lord and Saviour (Acts 2.41, 22.16).

5. In whose name must we be baptised?

Before His ascension, Jesus Christ gave to His disciples the order to baptise converts in the name of the Father, the Son and the Holy Spirit (Matthew 28.19). Is baptism in the name of Jesus valid? We will say yes, if this baptism means ""administered according to the teachings of Jesus", that is to say not opposed to baptism in the name of the Father, the Son and the Holy Spirit, recognising the baptism of Matthew 28. 19.

6. *What is the meaning of baptism?*
   Baptism has three meanings:
   1. Public testimony of faith in Jesus Christ, for the connection between baptism and faith comes out very clearly in Matthew 28.19, 16.15-16, Acts 2.41. Baptism follows faith, because it is only faith that saves. Baptism by water is a confession of faith in Jesus Christ, a commitment to God before men (1 Peter 3.21).
   2. Public testimony to the union of the believer with Christ in his death and resurrection; it is a visible sign of our spiritual immersion in Christ and of the regeneration brought about in us by the Holy Spirit (Romans 6.3-4).
   3. Public testimony of our membership of the church, that is to say the spiritual and universal community of those who profess faith in the same Lord (Ephesians 4.4-6).

Remarks: In some local churches baptism by water is a condition for taking Holy Communion. This obligation is not biblical, but recommended for reasons of order, for it is with baptism that most local churches list their effective membership.

7. *The water used for baptism:* Jesus Christ was baptised in the river Jordan, because he lived in Galilee. You can be

baptised in any stream, river, lake, pond, swimming pool, provided you are entirely bathed in the water.

Who has the right to baptise? One who has received a mandate to baptise. In reality, any Christian can baptise, but for reasons of order, the Church gives a mandate to some people responsible for being busy with baptising, either a pastor, an elder or even a brother with a good testimony.

Chapter 7: The Holy Spirit

1 What the Holy Spirit is not
2 What He is
3 Different names and signs of the Holy Spirit
4 The work of the Holy Spirit
5 Baptism by the Holy Spirit
6 Being full of the Holy Spirit
7 Spiritual gifts and talents
8 Unction
9 The fruit of the Spirit

Chapter 7   The Holy Spirit

1. What the Holy Spirit is not: The Holy Spirit is not a thing, a force, a power, an influence. This bad interpretation of the Holy Spirit is part of a bad interpretation of Acts 1.8. The Bible says "You will receive a power, the Holy Spirit coming down on you, and you will be my witnesses...;" it is a matter of receiving a power when the Holy Spirit comes down; the Holy Spirit has a force, a power, and He manifests His presence in many ways.

2. *What He is:* The Holy Spirit is a real person, the third person of the Godhead, of the   Trinity, called also the Comforter (John 14.16-17); the Bible uses as its subject the personal pronoun, for in Greek the masculine pronouns are relative to human beings (John 14.16-17). He is a person; that is because it is not recommended to lie to, tempt, resist, sadden, or outrage the Holy Spirit (Acts 5.3,9; Acts 7.51, Ephesians 4.30, Hebrews10.29). When we talk of the Holy Spirit, we mean He is characterised by intelligence, capacity to know people and to resolve a moral problem; a sensitivity to the state of people's souls; and a willingness or capacity to decide on a course of action.

3. *Different names and symbols of the Holy Spirit:* The Holy Spirit is also called the Spirit of God, the Spirit of the Eternal, the Spirit of the living God, the Spirit of Jesus Christ, the Spirit of Christ, the Spirit of truth, the Spirit of life... (1 Corinthians 3.16, Isaiah 11.2, 2 Corinthians 3.3, Galatians 4.6, Philippians 1.19, Romans 8.9, John 16.13, Romans 8.2...). The Holy Spirit is represented by oil in the bestowal of Holy Unction creating gladness, a dove, fire, water, wind, a dewdrop, the mantle of Elijah, the

seal, a pledge… (John.3.34, Hebrews 1.9, Matthew 3.16, Acts 2.3, John 7.38-39, Ephesians 1.13-14, 4.30…).

4. *The work of the Holy Spirit:* The Bible shows us the work of the Holy Spirit in the Old and New Testaments. By the work of the Holy Spirit the Bible implies seeing the role which the Holy Spirit has played in creation and across the centuries.

4.1 The work of the Holy Spirit in the Old Testament: The personality and divinity of the Holy Spirit are shown by His works and attributes. The Holy Spirit is revealed as having taken part in the work of creation (Genesis 1.2). He is all-powerful and is present everywhere (Job 26.13, Psalms 104.30, 139.7). The Holy Spirit disputes with men (Genesis 6.3), He enlightens the mind and confers manual skills (Exodus 28.3, 31.3), He grants physical force (Judges 14.6, 19). The Holy Spirit makes some men capable of receiving and announcing divine revelations (Numbers 11.25, 2 Samuel 23.2). In the Old Testament the Holy Spirit comes onto the person whom He chooses, apparently without needing from that person any peculiar conditions, as in the New Testament. The Old Testament contains prophecies on the subject of a future effusion of the Spirit onto Israel (Exodus 37.14), as on "all flesh" (Joel 2.28-29).

4.2 The work of the Holy Spirit in the New Testament: In the Messiah:

a. At his conception and birth (Luke 1.34-35);

b. At His baptism: The Holy Spirit came down in the form of a dove, and John the Baptiser testified after His baptism that Jesus Christ has the Spirit without measure (Luke 3.22);

c. In His ministry, the Holy Spirit was at work (Acts 10.38);

d. In His death and resurrection (Romans 8.11, Ephesians 1.20) the Holy Spirit saw to it that the dead Christ would be resurrected from among the dead.

In sinful man: The Holy Spirit does a great work in sinful man, and also in the life of the Christian. He will prove people wrong about sin, of justice and of judgement (John 16.8). He convinces man of sin in a quiet way as to transgression against the law of God, of refusing to believe in Jesus. The Holy Spirit convinces men that they are unjust, sinners and worthy of condemnation until they accept the good man Jesus, who has taken the place of man on the cross; the Holy Spirit works by converting man to the Lord Jesus through new birth; but what does the Holy Spirit do around this new birth? It is the Holy Spirit who prepares the ground, convinces the heart of the sinner, gives to the sinner the taste of life in heaven, and contempt for life on earth. And it is the Holy Spirit who regenerates man. For regeneration is a new birth of the individual by the joint action of the word and the Holy Spirit (John 3.3-8, James 1.18). The person who is regenerated receives life eternal (1 John 5.12), becomes a child of God and shares the divine nature (2 Peter 1.4). He is declared to be justified in Christ, and is sealed by the Holy Spirit (1 Corinthians 1.30, Ephesians 1.13). The Holy Spirit changes our inclination, our source of rejoicing, our love, and He puts in us the will to please God. During the Christian journey the Holy Spirit helps the Christian to resist the desires of the flesh (Galatians 5.16-18), and He bears witness in us that we are children of God (Romans 8.16, John 3.24).

5 *Baptism by the Holy Spirit:* Baptism is an immersion or identification with Jesus. Baptism by the Holy Spirit is an immersion into the Spirit, a covering by the Holy Spirit (Acts 1.5). He comes into the conversion of some people, maybe after their conversion. Indispensable in the life of a Christian, baptism by the Holy Spirit gives us access to various spiritual gifts. Baptism by the Holy Spirit creates the body of Christ, in one way uniting believers with Jesus, and in another way assuring the unity of believers between themselves (1 Corinthians 12.13). There is only one baptism by the Spirit, but the Christian can be filled by the Holy Spirit many times.

6 *Being full of the Holy Spirit:* It is recommended to be full of the Holy Spirit (Ephesians 5.18). So that your cup runs over with the Holy Spirit, so the Lord wants to see us every day (Psalm 23.5). If the cup is only half full, the devil will seek to fill it in with bad things.

7 *Spiritual gifts (1 Corinthians 12).* A spiritual gift is a present received freely from the Holy Spirit. They are amenities from the Holy Spirit for building up the Church and accomplishing the work of God. The nine spiritual gifts are classified

The gifts of communication: the gift of prophecy, the gift of speaking in tongues, the gift of interpreting tongues;

The gifts of intelligence: the gift of wisdom, the gift of knowledge, the gift of discernment of spirits;

The gifts of power: the gift of faith, the gift of performing miracles, the gift of healing;

7.1 The gifts of communication: speaking in tongues (Mark 16.17, 1 Corinthians 14.4) prophecy – interpretation of tongues.

Speaking in tongues is a vocal miracle in which the Spirit of God manifests itself in man by using the vocal organs of man to speak to man in heavenly tongues. Speaking in tongues does not mean speaking in many languages or the science of learning many languages. And it does not have to be the subject of an ordinary initiation, but on the contrary spontaneous. These tongues may or may not be intelligible, either the languages of men or the languages of angels (Acts 2.8-11). While speaking in tongues, the Christian may pray, sing or communicate a message. If someone speaks in tongues and he or she interprets it, their message becomes a prophecy. The interpretation is useful only when speaking in tongues is communicated.

The gift of prophecy is different from the ministry of a prophet. Prophecy is the fact of communicating under divine inspiration, the will of God to men. One who has the gift of prophecy can be used by God to denounce sin, call men to repentance, inform rebels of their coming chastisement, announce the return of the Messiah, reveal hidden secrets, announce a blessing to someone or to the Church, edify and exhort the Church.

7.2 The gifts of intelligence: are gifts of knowledge or words of knowledge, gifts of wisdom, gifts of being able to discern spirits. These gifts are not a sum of teachings, of knowledge of the word of God that all Christians can have, but they are supernatural revelations of the knowledge of God that He communicates to man. Thanks to the *gift of knowing about people,* you can break the news of God's thoughts, wanting to heal someone of a specific illness.

The gift of wisdom (sometimes called the gift of intelligence) can help you solve a crucial problem in society or in the church; that was the case of Solomon before the women who disputed the ownership of a baby (1 Kings 3.16-23). It works along with the gift of knowing people.

The gift of discernment leads us into the spiritual world, so that we might detect the spirit which operates in a given circumstance (Acts 16.16-18).

7.3 The gifts of power: the gift of healing, the gift of faith, the gift of performing   miracles:

These are gifts by which God reveals His power in the world in general, and in the   Church in particular.

The gift of healing is not a medical science, nor is it spiritualism, but on the contrary a power of God which frees man from his illness. This gift heals not only natural diseases, but also supernatural illnesses. An illness not diagnosed, or declared incurable by the doctor, can be cured thanks to this gift. God equips most evangelists with this gift. Every Christian can cure an illness by prayer, but a person who has the gift of healing cures many illnesses at a time.

The gift of faith allows the person who is equipped with it not to recoil in front of a problem that is impossible to the naked eye. People who meet those who have the gift of faith treat them sometimes as fools or as people who have lost their reason. The gift often challenges, and makes a demonstration of the power of God.

The gift of miracles comes from God, while magic operates miracles that come from the devil. The gift of healing is different from the gift of performing miracles, for the first of these gifts concerns illnesses. Delivering someone from demons, from husbands of the night, is a miracle. The gift of miracles means that you can raise the dead, and make paralytics walk. The gifts of power are not given to Christians so that they can be proud of them. See that all may be done to the glory of God, and Him alone.

7.4 The difference between talents and gifts: A talent is a natural gift which is used for the glory of God, or for the glory of the devil. Spiritual gifts cannot be given to a pagan, while talents can be found among both pagans and Christians. Talents are manifested in different domains, such as the talent of singing, making conversation, discussing things, making and reciting poetry, the creative spirit, talent in sports, for example the talent of playing football. The Church must not stifle the talents of Christians, but on the contrary, organise them so that they serve the advancement of the work of God. A remark: The Church must speak of the Holy Spirit, of His gifts and the miracles of God if it wants to see the Holy Spirit at work. The Bible encourages Christians to aspire to the best gifts (1 Corinthians 14.1), and God promises to give us what our heart desires (Psalm 20.5).

8. Unction; anointing

8.1 Definition: It is the action of putting oil on to a person or on an object so as to sanctify them for a definite service.

Unction is a supernatural capacity that God gives to His servant to accomplish His supernatural acts.

8.2 Unction at the heart of history: In the Old Testament kings, priests offering sacrifices, and sometimes prophets were designated by unction (Exodus 30.22-33, 1 Samuel 10.1) for their investiture or consecration. Christ was anointed by the Spirit of God to accomplish His mission (Matthew 3.16, Acts 10.38). The Christian needs this unction to work efficiently. So that oil will not be lacking on your head, at all times read the Bible (Ecclesiastes 9.8, Psalm 23.5).

8.3 Who anoints? Is unction transmissible? Only God anoints or not either directly (Exodus 31.1-3), or by intervention of His servants during an official ceremony. Christ was anointed by God (Psalm 2.6); Joshua was anointed by Moses (Deuteronomy 34.9) and David by Samuel (1 Samuel 16.11-13).

8.4 Who can be anointed?

a) those who are called to a service or a particular ministry; all Christians chosen by God for a particular service; someone whom the Church wants to raise up for a particular service after being approved, and when their deeds speak of God. That can be done during an ordination;

b) all Christians who wish to be used powerfully by God; you need unction to preach well, to direct people and projects well, and even to work well in a factory making spare parts for example (1 Samuel 16.12-13, Exodus 31.1-3).

c) Unction for sick people (James 5.14); a very up-to-date practice in some countries, but avoided in others when occultists use the same practice. Unction for the sick is used to achieve the will of God, who demands this practice in the case of need; but this last practice must not be mystified. One must use ordinary oil, and if need be, use oil found at the house of the patient.

8.5 What does unction bring into the life of a Christian? Unction changes someone's destiny; in the case of David for instance, who changed from being a shepherd to becoming a king; unction brings elevation or glory into the ministry, as in the case of David again, who carried off a victory against Goliath, but do not be astonished to learn that glory will also bring you enmity. That was the case of David, who attracted to himself enmity from Saul; unction brings blessing, the taste of prayer, the fear of God...

9. The fruit of the Spirit (John 15.1-5, Galatians 5.22): it is inconceivable to be a Christian and not produce a fruit of the Spirit, but the Christian must seek to be attached to Jesus who is the vine (the trunk), so that we might produce lots of fruit. Christians who are vine shoots or branches must be evaluated with regard to their production of the fruit of the Spirit, and not according to spiritual gifts only. The fruits of the Spirit are love, joy, peace, patience, goodness, goodwill, faith, sweetness and self-mastery. In reality it is a fruit in many parts, and all Christians who wish to please God must have different parts of this fruit of the Spirit.

Chapter 8:   Reading the word of God

1 Definition and origin of the Bible

2 Author of the Bible

3 Subdivisions of the Bible

4 The presentation of different books

5 When, where and how to read the Bible

Chapter 8:   Reading the word of God; The Bible

1. *Definition and origin of the Bible:* The Bible is the word of God. Born in the desert countries of Sinai, the Bible is the most ancient and famous book. Translated into more than 2100 languages and dialects, and published in part or as a whole, in thousands of copies each year, the Bible is a best seller which has never gone out of print. It is a unique book in which God reveals Himself to man. It is a book which speaks of God, of peoples, of the history of the world, of the heart of man, of his soul and his thoughts. It is a book which fashions man, and it is a march of history towards eternity. The Bible is a book which presents things which have passed in time and space, and that in the most sincere way. Therefore it is a unique incarnation of universal truth. The Bible is the most widely read book, the most ancient and the most famous, presenting God, His relationships with Israel and humanity, the person of Jesus Christ, including His first arrival, His death for the salvation of humanity, His resurrection and His second coming. The first part of the Bible, called the Law, starts with Mount Sinai. The Bible says in Exodus 34.1, "The Eternal said to Moses, 'Cut two tablets of stone like the first ones, and I will write there words which were on the first tablets that you have broken.'"

2. *Author of the Bible:* God is the author of the Bible, in the sense that He has not only written Himself the Ten Commandments, He has also inspired the writers of this last work. Inspired by God Himself, and made up of 66 books, the Bible was written by about forty authors, and in the course of a period of more than fifteen centuries.

3. *Subdivision of the Bible:* Subdivided into two great parts: Old Testament and New Testament, the Bible is made of

a) *Old Testament (39 books):* five books that represent the Law or the Pentateuch (Genesis, Exodus, Leviticus, Numbers, Deuteronomy); twelve historical books (Joshua, Judges, Ruth, 1 and 2 Samuel, 1 and 2 Kings, 1 and 2 Chronicles, Ezra, Nehemiah and Esther); five poetical books which speak of the poetry of Wisdom (Job, Psalms, Proverbs, Ecclesiastes and the Song of Songs); seventeen prophetic books which speak of prophecy (Isaiah, Jeremiah, the Lamentations of Jeremiah, Ezekiel, Daniel, Hosea, Joel, Amos, Obadiah, Jonah and Micah, Nahum, Habbakuk, Zephaniah, Haggai, Zechariah and Malachi).

b) *New Testament (27 books):* four gospels (Matthew, Mark, Luke and John), which present Christ and His public ministry; one book of the Acts of the Apostles which displays the propagation of the Gospel of Jesus Christ; 21 books which explain the gospel of Jesus, and one book of the Apocalypse or the Revelation of St. John the Divine, which reveals the end of the world and the return of Christ.

4. *Presentation of the different books (author, theme and date of publication):*

Example: 1. Genesis: theme: the Commandments: creation of the heavens and the earth, vegetation, animals and man, origins of human institutions and relationships betwixt individuals. Date of publication: around 1450-1410 BC. Author: Moses.

5. *When, where and how to read the Bible:*

5.1 When and where to read the Bible? We want first of all to remind you that the Bible is the word of God; it is one of the ways, if not the most efficient way, that God uses to speak to us. We can read the Bible any time, provided that we learn something from it; in the morning because we are more disposed and less disturbed, and that before entertaining any activity: helps us to get orientated and ready for directives on the part of God for the day; in the evening before going to sleep, either during a session of family prayer or in the course of a daily evaluation of our different activities; at church during worship; during the break at school; during a journey by plane, train or lorry.

5.2 How to read the Bible? Have an appointment at a fixed hour each day with God; pray to God asking Him to help you to understand His word; read the Bible with care, using a commentary for reading the Bible which gives you a passage on which to meditate. Meditate and reflect on the text you are reading, referring to other versions of the Bible; choose the most beautiful verse or the words that speak most clearly to you; copy them into a notebook or into your diary; think about them during the day, and share them with the neighbours or a friend; pray, and turn into a prayer the words you have read; obediently put into practice what God has told you.

Remarks: it is important to follow a calendar established by specialists, for the simple reason that Biblical passages must be read in an ordered way so that at the end of a long period of time you might succeed in reading the entire Bible. It happens often that God sends you a passage of the Bible to meditate on; we encourage you to obey the Holy Spirit.

Reply during your reading of the Bible to certain questions, such as of what or of whom do these verses speak? Is there an example there to follow or not to follow? Is there an order to obey? Is there a promise for me, my family, my Church, my work, my nation? Is there something which God is showing me for which I must thank and praise Him or which I must ask Him about?

Chapter 9: How to manage one's health

1 General concept of health, about the human body
2 The position of God in our physical wellbeing
3 What to do to be in good health

Chapter 9: How to manage one's health

1. *A general idea of the health of the human body.*
Health, as defined by the World Health Organization
(WHO), is "a state of complete physical, mental and
social well-being and not merely the absence of
disease or infirmity."
There are very few people who know how to
appreciate the value of health, and even so it is on
that that the efficiency of our physical and mental
faculties depends. The body, an integral part of our
personality along with our minds and souls, is the seat
of our passions, feelings and impulses; we must
therefore keep it in perfect condition if we wish our
talents to be used.

2. *The position of God in our physical wellbeing:* The
Bible accords an important value to human health.
Many passages confirm this truth; for example
putting lepers in quarantine (Leviticus 13). One must
avoid touching dead bodies and the dead bodies of
animals (Leviticus 11.39). God's concern is to see
people prosper in all regards, and to be in good
health, just as the state of our soul prospers (3 John
v2). God wants to see us glorify Him in our bodies (1
Corinthians 6.19-20).

3. *What must we do to be in good health?* Accept that
God wants our physical wellbeing; believe that one
can always be in good health; believe in a divine cure
for all illnesses, even those which are declared
incurable; God needs your body to accomplish His will
for you; that is why we must take care of our health;
to know our bodies in order to maintain them in the

conditions needed to accomplish the God's work; it is desirable to manage your time; that is to say have sufficient time for sleep or rest, to think about an annual holiday or retreat, to do physical exercise compatible with the will of God; to avoid a food regime rich in fat; eat balanced meals: foods rich in carbohydrates – maize, rice, manioc, foods rich in proteins – meat, eggs, milk, fish, haricot beans, soya, peanuts and groundnuts; foods rich in vitamins and mineral salts (vegetables and fruits); drink water and avoid using alcohol or drugs.

Chapter 10:   Work, and material and financial prosperity

1 The origin of work, and God's thinking about work
2 You need big objectives to succeed in life
3 You must believe in material and financial blessing
4 You have to mix with those who believe in success
5 You have to manage your time

Chapter 10: Work, and material and financial prosperity

1. *The origin of work, and the thoughts of God on work:* "In the beginning God created the heavens and the earth (Genesis 1.1)," "and after six days of work God finished his work which He had done, and He rested on the seventh day from all His work (Genesis 2.2)." These two passages show us that God is a workman who does not neglect rest. In God's thinking man must work to eat and be happy, and that anyone who does not want to work has no right to have food to eat (Genesis 3.17, 2 Thessalonians 3.10).

2. *You need great objectives to succeed in life:* Before spending several years running after prosperity, spend some minutes or even hours defining the objectives linked to that prosperity. To succeed in life you need to outline its direction in answering the following questions: a) what do you want to do with your life? b) What will be your profession, trade or occupation? c) After following this career full time, are you planning on a second career? d) Where will you spend your retirement? e) Where will you spend eternity? All these questions are going to lead you to put up a list from which you must make a choice, acquiring skills and knowledge to achieve your objectives. But be warned: your objectives must have the following characteristics:

   Think deeply about your objectives, for your future depends on them. No-one other than yourself will be bothered about you. Your objectives must be credible first of all for yourself. You must believe in your objectives. Your objectives must be written down; your chosen objectives must be Specific, Measurable, Acceptable, Realistic and registered in Time (SMART!).

3. *You must believe in material and financial blessing:* God wants you to be prosperous and happy. It is Satanic to believe that the children of God must be poor throughout their lives. Some passages should convince badly informed Christians that this is not so:

a) Deuteronomy 28.13"The Eternal will be for you the head and not the tail".

b) Joshua 1.3"Every place where the sole of your foot treads I shall give you".

c) Psalm 60.14"With God we will make exploits: He will crush our enemies."(?)

d) Psalm 91.7 "If one thousand should fall beside you, and ten thousand on your right hand, you will not be wounded".

e) Proverbs 10.22 "It is the blessing of the Eternal God which enriches one, and He does not make any sorrow follow it".

f) Psalm 20.5 "We pray that He will give you what your heart desires, and that He will accomplish all your plans."

g) Matthew 28.20 "And behold, I am with you every day, until the end of the world"

4. *You must mix with people who believe in victory:* The Bible says in 1 Corinthians 15.33 "Be not deceived: bad company corrupts good manners". And he adds in Psalm 1.1 "Happy is the man who does not stand in the way of sinners, and who does not sit in the seat of

the scornful". Christians must select carefully their daily companions. From the fact that faith comes from what one hears, it is important that one should hear good words. Be aware of habitual pessimists, those who always say: "It will never work, similar plans have already been begun among us" or "If the plan works, it will not last one year". Remember the reply of Zerubbabel (Ezra 3.8, 4.1) and that of Nehemiah (Nehemiah 4.1-9) in front of their enemies during the reconstruction of the Temple and its walls. But who must we mix with to succeed? God, because He gives the best advice (Psalm 73.24); brothers and sisters in Christ who trust God and believe in His blessings and His miracles: the ancients, the old people who believe in divine victory.

5. *You must carefully manage your time:* Save for fixed objectives, you must learn to manage your time. It is desirable to have a diary or notebook where you can write in the five things that you plan to do tomorrow, and with precise times if possible. Plan what you will do in a month, a year or five years. Do not forget to insert rests, retirements, visits to family members or friends. Each night evaluate your success during the day, and trust the next day to the Lord Jesus, who is the master of your life.

Chapter 11:   Knowing how to give to God

1 Sacrifices

2 Offerings

3 Tithes

4 Collections, alms and gifts

5   What attitude to adopt when you make a gift. What to give- what it is that you receive by giving

6 What to give, whom to give it to, and when to give

Chapter 11:   Knowing how to give to God:

This entails thinking about giving your life, your body, your clothes, your money and your possessions. Many passages exhort us or ask us to give our life, our body and clothes (Matthew 16.25-26, Romans 12.1), or our money and goods (Deuteronomy 15.10, Proverbs 11.24). Since the days of the Old Testament God has always asked something from man, either sacrifice, an offering, a tithe, a collection, alms or gifts.

1. *Sacrifices:* Sacrifices are offerings of animals sacrificed to God. One can distinguish between
   a) Burnt offerings, or the sacrifice of an agreeable smell to the Eternal: blood was spread round the altar and on top of it, while the body of the animal was entirely burnt (Leviticus 1.1-9). It is a foretaste image of the sacrifice of Christ who was entirely delivered from death (Isaiah 53.10, John 10.17);
   b) The sacrifice of thanksgiving: an expression of recognition by man for blessings received, and a desire for communion with God. The part of the animal that was not burned was given back to the priests who offered the sacrifice and to the person who made the offering (Leviticus 3, 7.11-21, 1 Corinthians 10.16-18);
   c) The sacrifice of expiation: for the expiation and purification from sins so as to be welcomed by God, part of the blood was sprinkled on the tent or tabernacle. The body of the victim was burned outside of the camp (Leviticus 4.4-12, 6.22, Hebrews 2.17, 13.11-13);
   d) The sacrifice of guilt: for the expiation of and purification from sins committed unwillingly or in the material domain: in this case, a restitution of secret things was foreseen (Leviticus 5.14-26, Luke 19.8). All sacrifices

offered by the Levites were a foretaste of the perfect sacrifice of Christ Jesus (Hebrews 8.5, 10.1-18).

2. *Offerings:* That is gifts to God without blood being spilt. In the Old Testament they offered either fine wheat flour soaked in oil for making unleavened cakes (Leviticus 2.1-13)either the first fruits of the harvest (Leviticus 2.14-16, 23.10), or the tithes for the upkeep of the Levites (Numbers 18.21). Offerings are authorised in the new covenant, unlike the sacrifice of animals, which are already replaced by the expiatory death of Jesus Christ. They are offered during worship these days to meet the needs of the Church (to cover the costs of praise, bills for water and electricity, taxes and health treatments).

3. *Tithes:* Are one tenth of your income. It can be paid weekly or monthly, or even annually by Christian businesses. A promise is linked to the tithe. Malachi 3.10 says, "Take to the house of the Eternal God all your tithes so that there might be food in my house; put me to the test and you will see if I do not open to you the locks of heaven and if I do not spill on you blessings in abundance."

4. *Collections, alms and gifts:* A collection is an offering understood to be meeting a precise need, which must normally be explained to Christians (1 Corinthians 16.1-3), for example to support a missionary who wants to travel to the mission field, to pay the school or university fees of a brother in great difficulty, to organise a preaching mission. Alms are offerings for the poor, and God wants us to donate in total humility (Matthew 6.2). Gifts are voluntary offerings offered spontaneously and in an occasional way in recognition of the benefits sent from

the Lord, in favour of anyone (1 Corinthians 16.2), either in or outside of church.

5. *What attitude should we adopt when giving,* and why should we give? Also, what do we receive by giving?

Give to be blest, and give without regret. Deuteronomy 15.10 says "That your heart will not give with regret; for, because of that, the Eternal, your God, will bless you in all your work and in all your business."

Give to become richer. Proverbs 11.24 says "He who gives liberally becomes richer, and he who saves to excess grows poorer." Matthew 13.12 says "Wealth will be given to him who has, and it will be given in abundance." Malachi 3.10: "Take to the storehouse of the Eternal God all your tithes...then put me to the test...and you shall see if I shall not open the windows of heaven for you, and pour down for you an abundant blessing." 2 Corinthians 9.6: "Know this, that he who sows little shall reap little, but he who sows abundantly will reap abundantly".

6. *What should we give, and to whom should we give it?*

What to give? On the occasion of constructing the tabernacle the children of Israel brought what precious gifts they had. Exodus 35.32 says "Men as well as women came; all those whose hearts were well disposed brought buckles, rings, bracelets and all sorts of golden objects; each person brought the golden offering that had been consecrated to the Eternal God." Therefore we can give to God contributions for the advancement of His work; money, precious goods or even our intelligence, expertise and time.

To whom should we give? Since the time of the Old Testament offerings have been dedicated to God through the mediation of his priests. Apart from gifts and alms, which one can give to strangers through the Church, other offerings and gifts must be put in the offerings box at the local church. If that church has not yet formed a financial structure that functions efficiently, contributions must be given to the pastor.

What must you do if your local church is not concerned about your spiritual growth? You would be wrong to continue praying in that place where you cannot grow spiritually. In such a case, the tithe can be donated elsewhere; that is to say to those who are concerned with your spiritual growth or to missionary societies for example. We cannot finish this theme without warning the reader that there are Christians who do not like to give to the Church, but on the contrary finance with huge sums pagan activities; for example sport, friendly societies..., behaviour that God does not accept, because no blessing is kept for such actions (Haggai 1.5-11).

When to give? The Bible says, "He who sows abundantly will reap abundantly" (2 Corinthians 9.6), and it adds "From the morning sow your seed, and in the evening do not allow your hand to rest." It is important to be generous at every moment when the Holy Spirit compels you, and do so according to your ability.

Chapter 12:   Patriotism – the Christian patriot

1 Definition of the homeland
2 The position of the Bible on patriotism
3 The attitude of a Christian patriot

Chapter 12:   Patriotism – the Christian patriot

1. *Definition of the Fatherland or homeland:* The homeland is the country, province or town where one was born or where one has settled; lived for a very long period. Jeremiah 29:7 "Also, seek the peace and prosperity of the city to which I have carried you into exile. Pray to the LORD for it, because if it prospers, you too will prosper." A patriot is one who loves his or her country, who endeavours to serve it.   Patriots are individuals within a community, living on the same soil, united in respect of a cultural attachment in defence of what they value in life.

2. *The position of the Bible on patriotism:* The Bible, by means of the history of the children of Israel, supports and encourages patriotism.   God asks the children of Israel to love and defend their country (Exodus 10, Deuteronomy 28, Joshua 1).   Jesus Christ, in sending out the disciples on a mission, proves to us that He had a special love for His blood brothers, especially in noting their incredulity.   Take three examples:

2.1 In Matthew 10.5-8, Jesus orders the disciples "not to go towards non-Jews, and not to enter into the towns of Samaritans; go rather towards the lost sheep of the house of Israel."   That does not mean that Jesus Christ had come only for the Jews, because in John 4.42 the Bible describes the conversion to the Lord of several Samaritans.

2.2 Jesus Christ wept over Jerusalem, seeing that they could not believe that their Messiah had come, and he says in Luke 19.41-44, "As He approached the city, Jesus on seeing it, cried over it, and said, 'If you also, at least on this day which is given to you, knew the things which belonged to your peace!...It will come to you on the days when your enemies will surround you with trenches...They will destroy you, you and your children..., because you have not known the time of your visitation."

2.3. In the Acts of the Apostles 1.8, Jesus Christ says to His disciples, "You will be my witnesses in Jerusalem, in all Judea, in Samaria, and unto the uttermost parts of the earth." This order, used by Christ, has sometimes a patriotic meaning, proving His attachment.

3. *What must be the attitude of a Christian patriot?* The Christian patriot must believe in the prosperity of his country; pray for his country; manage the state, at any level of responsibility he is asked to accept, as if it was his own personnel; choose, in the case of an election, worthy representatives, of good morality, Christians believing in God and good managers; defend his country within the state as well as outside against all sorts of aggression – spiritual, physical, moral or economic; react against all ideologies or conceptions tending to destroy the faith based on Jesus Christ the Son of God; involve himself so that his country might know the Lord Jesus, who is the only true solution and the only remedy against the sufferings of humanity; make for a healthy environment, by being watchful over the cleanliness of his house, his street, his area, his town and his country; being hospitable in safeguarding the interests of people who live in the nation.

Chapter 13:   Sanctification

Chapter 13:   Sanctification

1. *Definition:* Sanctification in both the Old and New Testaments, as well as derivative words, come from the Hebrew Qodesch and the Greek Hagios, which mean in a general sense "put apart for God", "separation", "made holy".   These words "sanctification," "sanctified" and "holy" are applied to both people and objects. Sanctification can mean

a) making holy, purified, put aside for God, consecrated by people for a special service for the Lord, as in the case of sacrificial priests in Exodus 29.1-7, 1 Chronicles 23.13;

b) consecrating or sanctifying objects or days as in the case of the sanctified altar and the objects in the tabernacle (Exodus 29.36-37, 30.26-29);

c) purifying oneself, separating one's self from all that is evil (Exodus 19.22, Joshua 3.5, 1 Peter 1.15-16);

d) glorifying and honouring the name of the Eternal God (Isaiah 58.13, 8.13, Matthew 6.9).

2. *The importance of sanctification:* Sanctification has a considerable place in the life of a Christian, because the Bible tells us in Hebrews 12.14 that without it no-one can see God.   It is the will of God that His children should be sanctified (1 Thessalonians 4.3, 5.23). Sanctification is a gift from God, grace from the Lord, and it must be accepted, desired and exercised.

3. *By what means we can be sanctified:* We can be sanctified by the word of God (John 17.17); the blood of Christ (Hebrews 13.12, 1 John 1.7-9); divine chastisement and correction (Hebrews 12.10-11); our attachment or abandonment to the Lord, for our

sanctification is proportional to our communion with the Lord, and our obedience to direction from the Holy Spirit (Romans 6.15-19, 2 Corinthians 7.1, Titus 2.11-14, 1 Samuel 15.22).

4. *Stages of our sanctification:*

a) immediate sanctification, which is instantaneous, for it happens during your conversion (1 Corinthian s 6.11, Ephesians 6.18). Those who have converted to the Lord are considered holy, sanctified from the moment when they first believed (Philippians 1.1, Hebrews 3.1);

b) progressive sanctification: those who believe after their conversion undergo the experience of sanctification by the action of the Holy Spirit, either by means of the Scriptures or through an internal conviction (John 17.17, 2 Corinthians 3.18, Ephesians 5.25-26). This sanctification is continual after one's conversion (2 Corinthians 7.1, Colossians 3.5-10). Progressive sanctification expects a manifest will on the part of the believer. It is a way of responding to the demand of the Lord in Revelation 22.11b, who says "He who is holy still sanctifies himself;"

c) final and complete sanctification will take place on the return of the Lord at His second coming (1 Thessalonians 5.23, 1 John 3.2, Ephesians 5.27, 1 John 3.2). To conclude, sanctification must be accepted, desired and exercised, for without it no-one shall see the Lord. And our evaluation of someone as a Christian must not be based solely on their display of spiritual gifts, but also on the holiness of the believer.

Chapter 14:   Waiting for the return of Jesus Christ

1 The first coming of Jesus Christ
2 The second coming of Jesus Christ
3 When is He expected?
4 The signs
5 By which country will Christ return?

Chapter 14:   Waiting for the return of Jesus Christ

1. *Jesus Christ's first coming; The* news about Jesus Christ in the Old Testament is clear, but sometimes it presented the coming of a Messiah who would suffer and be rejected (Isaiah 53) or the coming of a triumphant Messiah (Isaiah 9.5, 11.1-2). Prophecies about the coming of a Messiah are so real that it would be insensitive not to believe them.   For example: He would be born of a virgin.

1. That is why the Lord Himself will give us a sign; here the virgin would become pregnant, she would give birth to a son, and she would give him the name Emmanuel (Isaiah 7.14). The Messiah would be born for all humanity and He would be powerful and eternal.

2. For unto us a child is born, unto us a son is given, and authority will rest upon his shoulders; they will call Him Wonderful, Counsellor, the mighty God, Eternal Father, and Prince of Peace (Isaiah 9.6). He would be born in Bethlehem, a town in Judah.

3. "And you, Bethlehem of Ephratah, small among the thousands of Judah, from you shall one come forth for me who will rule over Israel, whose goings forth go back to ancient times, to the days of eternity (Micah 5.1). He will take away the sins and woes of humanity.

4. However, these are sufferings that He has born for us; it is our pains with which He is loaded: and we thought He was punished, struck by God, and humiliated. But he was wounded for our sins, broken for our iniquities, and the chastisement which gives us

peace has fallen upon Him, and it is by His bruises that we have been healed (Isaiah 53.4-5).

The accomplishment of prophecies:

He was actually born in Bethlehem (Luke 2.1-7), and cured illnesses (Luke 8.41-55). He announced His death and His resurrection (Luke 9.22), He died on the cross (John 19.16-18), and rose again from among dead (Mark 16.1-7), and finally was taken up into heaven (Luke 24.49-53).

He had promised to return:

Acts 1.8-11 says, "And you will be my witnesses in Jerusalem, in all Judea, in Samaria, and unto the farthest reaches of the earth." After saying that, as they were looking, He was taken up, and a cloud hid Him from their eyes. And as their eyes were fixed on heaven as He went, two men dressed in white appeared to them, and said, "Men of Galilee, why do you stop to look into heaven? This Jesus, who was taken up into heaven from among you, will come in the same manner as you have seen Him go into heaven."

2.The second coming of Jesus Christ: The return of Christ concerns the faith of the Church, of Israel, and of the nations.

2.1The Lord's raising: Concerning the Church, the coming of the Lord was called the Raising. The Bible says in John 14.3, "And, when I shall come there, and will have prepared a place for you, I shall come again, and i shall take you with me, so that there where I am you will be also." And in 1 Thessalonians 4.16-17, the Bible says "For the Lord Himself, at a given signal, at the voice of an archangel, and at the sound of the trumpet of God, will come down from heaven, and those who died in Christ will be the first to be raised from the dead. Then we who are alive, that are left, shall altogether with them be caught up on the clouds, to meet the Lord in the air, and thus we shall always be with the Lord. During this taking away, the Lord will come again from heaven to take His Church, which is to say those who have believed in the Lord. Those who have died in Christ will rise from the dead, and will receive an incorruptible body and Christians who are still alive will be transformed and will receive an incorruptible body (1 Corinthians 15.51-55).

2.2: The return of the Lord for Israel: For Israel, the return of the Lord Jesus to earth will mark the accomplishment of prophecies concerning its national assembly, its conversion, then its reestablishment in peace and with power, according to the covenant made with David (2 Samuel 7.16, Zachariah 14.1-9).

2.3: The return of the Lord for the nations: For the nations, the return of the Lord Jesus will carry away the destruction of the current world political system (Daniel 2.34-35) and the judgement described in Matthew 25.31-46; we are present during this return at the last judgement, at the separation of the just and the unjust. The just will take possession of the kingdom of God, and the unjust will be thrown into the eternal fire which has been prepared for the devil and his angels.

3. At what date is His return expected?

The Bible says in Mark 13.35 "Watch out therefore, for you do not know at what hour the master of the house will come, whether at the onset of darkness or during the middle of the night, or at cockcrow or in mid-morning. For of the day or the hour no-one knows, neither the angels of heaven or the Son, but only the Father" (Matthew 24.36). And in Revelation 22.20 the Lord says that He will come soon.

4. What are the signs?

-wars, international disquiet, famines, epidemics, persecutions, false Messiahs, apostasy...
- the accomplishment of ancient prophecies about Israel, as to the development of the nation of Israel, its conversion to Christianity, waiting for the Messiah, thoughts on the reconstruction of the Temple,
- globalisation, single currency,
- the spread of the gospel.

5. In which country will Christ reveal Himself?

As for the "Raising", Christ will not arrive on the earth, but from the air, as with the help of a magnet he will attract all Christians. As for His return for the nations, the Bible says in Zacharias 14.4 that "His feet will land on that day on the mount of Olives, which is opposite to Jerusalem, beside the east; the mount of Olives will be split in the middle. To the east and to the west, and a great valley will be formed; half of the mount will move towards the north, and half towards the south." Some researchers already indicate a fissure inside this Mount of Olives, situated to the East of Jerusalem.

6. *What attitude must we adopt in the face of Jesus Christ's return?* Christians must
   – keep watch with irreproachable behaviour, since they know not the day nor the hour of His coming (Matthew 25.13);
   - console themselves, despite their afflictions and persecutions here on earth (1 Thessalonians 4.17-18);
   - bring the gospel to pagans, knowing their dreadful fate (Matthew 25.31-33, 41);
   - work more and more for the Lord in view of the rewards reserved for them (1 Corinthians 15.58, Daniel 12.3).

Conclusion

After having run through these topics, the Christian has no more right to a puny belief. On the contrary lead a victorious and balanced Christian life; that is what we call a successful life in Christ Jesus. From now on the Christian will no more be a child, floating and carried away by every wind of doctrine, by the mistakes of men and by their cunning, but by the grace of God he or she will be able to work more and more for the Church and the society in which he or she lives.

Who is Dr Hubert Kayonda Ngamaba

Dr Hubert Kayonda is pastor of the Ephrata Church in the city of Bolton and works for the University of York. Graduated in Practical Theology, Dr Kayonda is a speaker whom God uses powerfully in his local Church, on radio and television. Hubert Kayonda is married to Madame Fideline since April 1994 and they have five children: Esperant, Elgracia, Esther, Elysee and Benedict. Hubert and Fideline are a blessing for the Church and the nations. Kayonda has a background in health psychology and mental health research. Dr Kayonda is actually working within a team in the Social Policy and Social Work Department to evaluate social interventions within Community Mental Health Team. Prior to joining the University of York, Dr Kayonda worked for the NHS (Greater Manchester Mental Health) and the University of Manchester on several projects. Dr Kayonda has a BSc (Hons) in Psychology and Counselling from the University of Bolton, Masters in International Development and PhD in Psychology from the University of Manchester. Dr Kayonda has published high-quality research papers in several academic journals including the European Journal of Public Health, Journal of Mental Health, Religion & Culture, Journal of Psychology in Africa, Journal of Religion and Health, and Quality of Life Research.

It is in trying to help our brothers and sisters grow normally that we wanted to put at the disposal of Christians a series of Biblical teachings for today. Faith comes from what one hears; that is why, after conversion the Christian must try and listen to good spiritual things, balanced and presented by Christians who have not only spiritual knowledge but also a training and occupation other than the pastorate.

Many themes have been elaborated in our manual, beginning with redemption, new birth, conversion to the Lord Jesus, spiritual beings and spiritual warfare, the Church and the fellowship, bearing witness, baptism by water, the Holy Spirit, reading the word of God, achieving physical and moral health, work, as well as material and financial prosperity, knowing how to give, love of one's country, sanctification, and finally the return of Jesus Christ. These subjects are not the subjects of classic courses at a Bible college, but are useful matters for a new convert in a formative stage; why not for a former convert who wants a victorious life in Christ Jesus.